Little People, **BIG DREAMS**™

PABLO PICASSO

Written by
Maria Isabel Sánchez Vegara

Illustrated by
Teresa Bellón

Frances Lincoln
Children's Books

In the sunny city of Malaga, Spain, lived a little boy called Pablo. He could draw before he even learned how to talk. Instead of "mom" or "dad," his first word was "lápiz," which means pencil in Spanish.

ESPETOS

Don José, his father, was an art teacher. He taught his son how to use oil paints. Pablo was just nine when he completed his first painting: a man riding a horse in a bullfight.

He was only a kid, but was already a better artist than his dad!

His father took him to Madrid to visit its most famous museum: El Prado. Pablo hoped that his paintings would one day be hanging on the walls, next to the work of great Spanish masters like Goya or Velázquez.

He attended a well-known art school in Barcelona, and soon he mastered almost every known style. Still, Pablo didn't want to paint like grown-ups did hundreds of years ago. He wanted to show the world his own way!

Pablo's first solo exhibition was held in a café called The Four Cats, a place where painters and poets would hang out. There, he met his friend Carles. They were very different, but instantly they became buddies. Soon, they were sharing a tiny studio.

When he visited Paris, the center of the art scene, Pablo knew it was the perfect place to settle. But the world wasn't ready for his style and making a living as an artist was hard. Sometimes, he burned his own paintings to keep his room warm.

One day, he got terrible news: his dear Carles had died.
For a long time, Pablo would only use the color blue
in his paintings. It was his way of letting everyone know
how sad and lonely he felt after the loss of his friend.

But luckily, sadness never lasts forever! And after two long years of feeling blue, Pablo's paintings were filled with color again. He used red, pink, and orange to paint the clowns, dancers, and acrobats he saw at the circus and cabarets.

With a friend and artist called Georges, he created a whole new style: Cubism. They painted one thing from many different angles, and put it all together in the same picture. The result was as playful as a little kid's drawing.

The day Georges brought a roll of wallpaper to their studio, Pablo couldn't wait to start experimenting with it. He cut up pieces of it and pasted them onto his painting. It was the first time collage was used in a work of art.

Pablo was a well-known artist when war broke out in Spain. He created a huge black and white painting that showed the bombing of a town called Guernica. It was the most moving anti-war painting the world had ever seen.

For him, one idea could be expressed in lots of ways. He kept exploring different styles, materials, and techniques all his life. Pablo created so many paintings and sculptures that his art could fill a whole museum!

And even though it took him just four years to paint like a master, little Pablo never stopped trying to paint like a child. Because all children are artists— we just need to keep believing it once we grow up.

PABLO PICASSO

(Born 1881 – Died 1973)

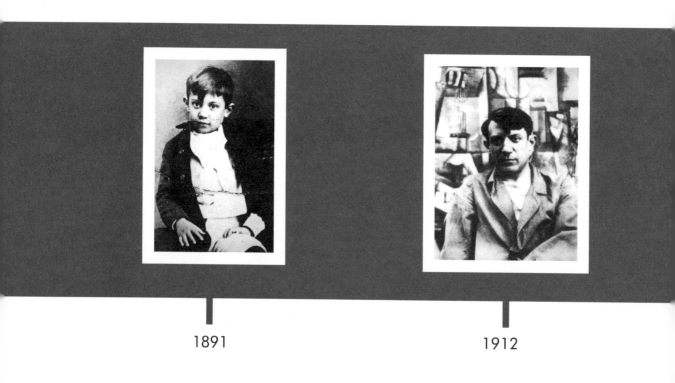

1891   1912

Pablo Ruiz Picasso was born on 25th October 1881 in Malaga, Spain. After the death of his 7-year-old sister, the family moved to Barcelona, where Pablo's father taught art. Under the guidance of his father, Pablo went to art school at the age of 16. But he felt pressured by his family and found formal education too restrictive—he was much more inspired by the world he saw around him. Pablo decided to quit school and began studying art in his own way. In 1900, he had his first solo exhibition and met Carles Casagemas. Together they moved to Paris, the center of the art scene, and Pablo remained in France for the majority of his life. When Carles died in 1901, Pablo grieved through his art for two years—known as his Blue Period—before he began to paint using vibrant colors again as part of

1936

1965

his Rose Period. In 1907, he created a new style of art called Cubism with fellow artist, Georges Braque. This style, in which objects were painted from different perspectives then combined into one image, changed art forever, and inspired many subsequent creative movements. From then on, Pablo was seen by the public as being a revolutionary artist. Throughout his life, he created thousands of artworks, from paintings and sculptures to ceramics and rugs, made with all kinds of different materials. With his eclectic style, Pablo contributed significantly to the development of modern art in the 20th century, making him one of the most influential artists that the world has ever seen. His story teaches us that even when things get tough, we should all believe in our own talents.

Want to find out more about **Pablo Picasso?**

Have a read of this great book:

Who was Pablo Picasso? by True Kelley

If you're in Barcelona, Spain, you can see some
of Pablo's work at the Picasso Museum.

Brimming with creative inspiration, how-to projects, and useful information to enrich your everyday life, Quarto Knows is a favourite destination for those pursuing their interests and passions. Visit our site and dig deeper with our books into your area of interest: Quarto Creates, Quarto Cooks, Quarto Homes, Quarto Lives, Quarto Drives, Quarto Explores, Quarto Gifts, or Quarto Kids.

Text © 2021 Maria Isabel Sánchez Vegara. Illustrations © 2021 Teresa Bellón.

Original concept of the series by Maria Isabel Sánchez Vegara, published by Alba Editorial, s.l.u.

Little People, Big Dreams and Pequeña & Grande are registered trademarks of Alba Editorial, s.l.u. for books, printed publications, e-books and audiobooks. Produced under licence from Alba Editorial, s.l.u.

First Published in the UK in 2021 by Frances Lincoln Children's Books, an imprint of The Quarto Group.

The Old Brewery, 6 Blundell Street, London N7 9BH, United Kingdom.

T 020 7700 6700 **www.QuartoKnows.com**

All rights reserved.

A catalogue record for this book is available from the British Library.

ISBN 978-0-7112-5950-8

Set in Futura BT.

Published by Katie Cotton • Designed by Sasha Moxon

Edited by Lucy Menzies • Production by Nikki Ingram

Editorial assistance from Rachel Robinson

Manufactured in Guangdong, China CC102021

1 3 5 7 9 8 6 4 2

Photographic acknowledgements (pages 28-29, from left to right): MALAGA - SPAIN 1891: Pablo Picasso at 10 years old on 1891 in Malaga, Spain, Picasso's native city. © API/Gamma-Rapho via Getty Images 2. PABLO PICASSO (1881-1973). /nSpanish painter and sculptor. Picasso before his canvas, "The Aficionado,"; shortly after it was completed in the summer of 1912. © Granger Historical Picture Archive / Alamy Stock Photo 3. Photo Portrait 1936 Pablo Picasso (1881–1973 Spain Spanish) by Rogi Andre 1900-1970 Hungary Hungarian © Peter Horree / Alamy Stock Photo 4. France. Spanish painter Pablo Picasso. Reproduction. © ITAR-TASS News Agency / Alamy Stock Photo

Collect the Little People, BIG DREAMS™ series:

FRIDA KAHLO

COCO CHANEL

MAYA ANGELOU

AMELIA EARHART

AGATHA CHRISTIE

MARIE CURIE

ROSA PARKS

AUDREY HEPBURN

EMMELINE PANKHURST

ELLA FITZGERALD

ADA LOVELACE

JANE AUSTEN

GEORGIA O'KEEFFE

HARRIET TUBMAN

ANNE FRANK

MOTHER TERESA

JOSEPHINE BAKER

L. M. MONTGOMERY

JANE GOODALL

SIMONE DE BEAUVOIR

MUHAMMAD ALI

STEPHEN HAWKING

MARIA MONTESSORI

VIVIENNE WESTWOOD

MAHATMA GANDHI

DAVID BOWIE

WILMA RUDOLPH

DOLLY PARTON

BRUCE LEE

RUDOLF NUREYEV

ZAHA HADID

MARY SHELLEY

MARTIN LUTHER KING JR.

DAVID ATTENBOROUGH

ASTRID LINDGREN

EVONNE GOOLAGONG

BOB DYLAN

ALAN TURING

BILLIE JEAN KING

GRETA THUNBERG

JESSE OWENS

JEAN-MICHEL BASQUIAT
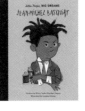

ARETHA FRANKLIN

CORAZON AQUINO

PELÉ

ERNEST SHACKLETON

STEVE JOBS

AYRTON SENNA

LOUISE BOURGEOIS

ELTON JOHN

JOHN LENNON

PRINCE

CHARLES DARWIN

CAPTAIN TOM MOORE

HANS CHRISTIAN ANDERSEN

STEVIE WONDER

MEGAN RAPINOE

MARY ANNING

MALALA YOUSAFZAI

ANDY WARHOL

RUPAUL

MICHELLE OBAMA

MINDY KALING

IRIS APFEL

ROSALIND FRANKLIN

RUTH BADER GINSBURG

MARILYN MONROE

KAMALA HARRIS

ALBERT EINSTEIN

CHARLES DICKENS

YOKO ONO

MICHAEL JORDAN

NELSON MANDELA

PABLO PICASSO

ACTIVITY BOOKS

STICKER ACTIVITY BOOK

COLORING BOOK

LITTLE ME, BIG DREAMS JOURNAL

Discover more about the series at www.littlepeoplebigdreams.com